D1738969

Ross's

Novel Discoveries

Michael Ross

Ross's

Novel Discoveries

Michael Ross

Michael Ross

Rare Bird • Los Angeles, Calif.

This is a Genuine Rare Bird Book

A Rare Bird Book | Rare Bird Books
453 South Spring Street, Suite 302
Los Angeles, CA 90013
rarebirdbooks.com

FIRST HARDCOVER EDITION

Set in Minion
Printed in the United States
Distributed in the US by Publishers Group West

Publisher's Cataloging-in-Publication data

Ross, Michael.
Ross' Novel Discoveries : Quotes from Great Works on Men, Women, Romantic Relationships, Love, Sex, and Marriage/by Michael Ross.
pages 152
ISBN 978-1-942600-03-9

1. Quotations, English. 2. Love—Quotations, maxims, etc. 3. Sex—Quotations, maxims, etc. 4. Man-woman relationships—Quotations, maxims, etc. 5. Marriage—Quotations, maxims, etc. I. Title.

PN6231.L6 R66 2015
809/.933543—dc23

To my wife, Virginia, with love

Introduction

My credentials for offering this collection of quotations are twofold. The reader may consider one or the other more important. I hope that at least one qualifies me to offer these quotations with some credibility.

The first is my experience reading literature. I grew up seeing both my father and mother reading at every opportunity. This may have led, in part, to my majoring in English in college. I will admit, however, that another important factor was learning before declaring my major that English seemed to have the fewest required courses both inside and outside of the requirements of the major. Although I enjoyed many of the courses, even Victorian literature and modern and contemporary poetry, I confess that I, along with quite a few of my classmates, did not read all the assigned books. Somehow I made my way through exams and papers with modest success despite my lack of diligence.

I began reading in earnest during my four years (and one day) in the Navy, which immediately followed graduation from college. (My commitment was four years, and I had planned to see if I could get out a day early before I learned that serving one day more than four years would allow me to cash out my unused leave as a lieutenant over four years and would generate a much higher payment.) There was often little else to occupy the time at sea; my tours of duty included one roundtrip across the Pacific Ocean and two across the Atlantic Ocean, along with a couple of trips to and from Guantanamo Bay. I suppose my exposure to literature in high school and college led me to read higher-quality books than I otherwise might have selected.

My reading for pleasure continued through law school, even during exam periods, and my legal career. Once I got going, it was impossible to stop. As this collection is being submitted for publication,

I have read approximately 1,100 books, mostly fiction by well-regarded authors. (I should confess that I keep a log of the books I have read.) Most of my reading has been of modern and contemporary American authors, but I have read quite a few British novels, and plays, and a variety of works by a number of European, Latin American, and Asian authors. I have also made it a practice periodically to read or reread classics.

The second is my experience with romantic relationships. Looking back, it seems that I had a knack for burning through girlfriends, and later, lady friends, at quite a pace. It started with a couple of steadies in high school, slowed considerably during my four years at an all-male college in the late sixties (I did not know when I committed to attend that women came to party only on "big weekends") and during my naval career in the early seventies, but picked up, and maybe made up for lost opportunities, thereafter. These relationships varied in duration from fairly long-term to quite short-term, and included engagement to one fine young lady twice (the wedding invitations were printed but not mailed each time), and one marriage that ended in divorce after only a few years. If I learned anything of value during these relationships, it was too late to salvage them. Nonetheless, I have now been happily married for more than twenty-two years, a personal best in duration for me, but for which the credit goes to my wife.

Sometime during all this reading, I started collecting quotes on a wide variety of topics, several of which are included in this book. In each quote, something the narrator wrote, or a character said, or thought, jumped off the page at me. As the collection grew, I became very interested in sharing them. Readers will agree with some quotes and disagree with others, but my aim is to amuse, entertain, and provoke, not to espouse a point of view.

It will become apparent that many of the quotations would fit in a different section. There is some natural connection between or among these topics, and I had to make some tough decisions on a number of the quotes. If my choices have not been the best, I apologize in advance.

Quotations are useful in several ways: They can be inspirational for the reader alone. Some are candidates for sharing with a loved one, friend, or even an ex-lover. I often send what I think, or hope, are relevant quotes to our nineteen-year-old son and our seventeen-year-old daughter. I have no idea if they take any of them to heart, but, at least, they do not complain about my practice. Geoffrey O'Brien wrote in the March 31, 2013, edition of *The New York Times* that "We Are What We Quote," but even if we are not, I think many of these quotations will be useful, interesting, or fun for you, reader.

Men and Women

Although volumes of nonfiction have been written about the differences between men and women (and probably far less on what they have in common), authors of fiction—directly and less directly, through their characters—have made some very quotable observations about men and women. Fiction allows authors the opportunity to weigh in as narrator and to have characters express a variety of views.

It will be apparent that the authors quoted here are predominantly male, so even their female characters' views may be tainted by a male perspective. Despite this bias, many male authors and their characters have some less-than-complimentary comments on men.

Here is an example from a highly-regarded storyteller:

...a lot of grown men play sports games out in their heads, in which they are always a superhero. That's the only way they can accomplish what they can't do in real life.

Leon Uris, Mitla Pass

Another author whose novels are very popular has a more complex, but still unflattering, commentary:

«»

All men contain several men inside them, and most of us bounce from one self to another without ever knowing who we are. Up one day and down the next; morose and silent in the morning, laughing and cracking jokes at night.

Paul Auster, The Brooklyn Follies

A recurring theme is the admission that men do not understand women. One assumes that women understand men much better. A prominent Southern author put it this way:

«»

Women are mythical creatures. They have no more connection with the ordinary run of things than do centaurs.

Walker Percy, *Love in the Ruins*

This sentiment is echoed by a prolific writer of several novels in a variety of genres, and he puts it quite succinctly:

«»

Women are incalculable.

Gore Vidal, Creation

One of my favorite authors uses this example to illustrate men's lack of understanding:

《》

Men are worthless; they always think the issue is what's at issue.

Richard Powers, Galatea 2.2

So when it comes to describing women, is it any wonder that women are in for a great deal of criticism? A very popular contemporary author's character explains one way in which he thinks women differ from men:

《》

Women, generally speaking, had a lot of needs. They needed to stay in nice places, and needed to pee every time you turned around, and needed to keep you abreast of what they were thinking pretty much constantly.

Richard Russo, Empire Falls

A Nobel Prize-winning author's character explores another alleged difference this way:

«»

Fact is, women over-elaborate everything and make life twice as complicated as any normal man ever would, and then they kick because the men don't jump in and kill themselves taking care of things they never wanted in the first place.

Sinclair Lewis, *The Prodigal Parents*

If there were any merit to that accusation, then the next one, in a novel by a prominent British author, about difficulties in communications, might make sense:

《》

...in the human or material sphere the nearest comparable disparity [to the million words written for every word in the Bible] was between the number of words that women said and the number that would have to have been said about what they had said in order to produce a full or clear or straight account of any matter.

Kingsley Amis,
The Folks That Live on the Hill

Further evidence of male misunderstanding comes from a very highly regarded female author whose male character makes an interesting observation:

《》

[He] thought girls must actually enjoy crying, the way they kept dwelling on what made them sad.

Anne Tyler, *If Morning Ever Comes*

So, it would not be surprising if these failures of understanding and communications lead to some bad feelings. One very popular contemporary author's character expresses his frustration this way:

«»

If there was one thing Bech resented about women, it was the way they so rapidly forgave themselves for the hysteria they inflicted on others.

John Updike, Bech is Back

Another of my favorite contemporary authors has his character opine that all these issues may have begun much younger, that is, with boys and girls:

«»

That's how it is with boys, you know that. Always looking at girls, always sizing them up, always hoping to run into the knockout beauty who will suck the breath out of you and make your heart stop beating.

Paul Auster, *Man in the Dark*

The famous author of a classic commentary on youth puts it even more forcefully, albeit from a different slant:

《》

That's the thing about girls. Every time they do something pretty, even if they're not much to look at, or even if they're sort of stupid, you fall half in love with them, and then you never know where the hell you are. Girls. Jesus Christ. They can drive you crazy. They really can.

J. D. Salinger, The Catcher in the Rye

But, boys and girls grow up. Or do they? Another Nobel Prize-winning author summarizes this difference between men and women:

«»

The ones who truly grow up,...are no good because men are either children or old— there is nothing in between. But in their childlike unreason and irresponsibility there is sometimes greatness. Please understand that I know most women are more intelligent, but women grow up, women face realities—and women are very rarely great.

John Steinbeck,
The Short Reign of Pippin IV

Regardless of how young or old it started, much has been made of the contrasts between men and women. Steinbeck's character describes one difference this way:

《》

There is no doubt that every woman needs another woman now and then as an escape valve for the pressures of being a woman. For her the man's releases are not available, the killing of small or large animals, vicarious murder from a seat at the prize ring.

John Steinbeck,
The Short Reign of Pippin IV

Another of my favorite contemporary authors describes very concisely a more fundamental difference:

《》

Women, unlike men, actually notice things.

Richard Russo, Bridge of Sighs

A character in this novel notes an important advantage that women may have over men:

《》

Women are sharp about sexual attraction, even when they themselves are not involved. All their senses are trained to detect the beginnings of interest and inclination, a man's loss of neutrality.

V. S. Naipaul, *Magic Seeds*

But, the differences may manifest themselves in very seemingly insignificant ways:

«»

Why do women's footsteps always sound more aggressive than men's? It can't be just the high heels; it must be an energy, a pouncingness, in the gender.

John Updike, *Roger's Version*

Romantic Relationships

One might conclude that even if only some of the differences between men and women described above were true, the prospects for a mutually satisfying (or better) relationship appear slim. On the other hand, maybe it is these and other differences that make successful, happy relationships possible. After all, would men and women want the opposite sex to be all that much like themselves? So, despite, or because of, the differences, men and women develop relationships for better or worse, as the saying goes. Some survive and some dissolve, in each case for a variety of reasons. It is, therefore, no small wonder that literature is full of commentary on romantic relationships.

In some cases, men may simply not be able to survive without a woman. A prolific British humorist weighs in on this topic:

And he was so helpless, so vulnerable, so essentially the sort of man who, without a woman's hand to guide him, must inevitably trip over his own feet and plunge into one of life's numerous morasses.

P. G. Wodehouse, The Girl in Blue

And, even if he were to survive, life might be challenging, at best, without a woman. Here is a very concise admission by a character in a novel:

«»

Life without a woman to temper your stupidities was difficult indeed.

Jim Harrison, The Great Leader

Some men may be interested in but uncertain about women. This commentary may be apt even though women no longer always wear dresses, and their modern wardrobe may increase the uncertainty:

«»

Whenever a man met confusion in this life, it almost always wore a dress.

Ivan Doig, *Prairie Nocturne*

Efforts to explain away the confusion may be futile. Here, a character wants to try but finds the task daunting:

«»

He would have liked to tell his nephew that men and women were shadows, and shadows within shadows, to one another.

Saul Bellow, *The Dean's December*

Despite the lack of understanding, many a man makes an effort to meet and woo women, often without success. Is this assessment on target?

«»

Men are never more foolish or absurd than when they "make a pass."

V. S Naipaul, *Magic Seeds*

When a man reaches the point of wanting a woman's love, he may not pursue the best way of finding it or understanding how he got it:

«»

They [men] like to believe they can win a woman's love through charm and seduction. They like to imagine, if they are ever so fortunate to gain, however briefly, the love of a half-decent woman, that somehow they earned it. By words and deeds and skills. And, of course, that is what causes the rapid demise of so many otherwise possibly adequate relationships: that, like politicians, men are deeply and supremely self-contemptuous. Therefore, the urgency of assigning self-contempt through becoming worthy of love in the eyes of another. But therein lies the inevitability of disappointment. Just as politicians develop a deep contempt for anyone crazy enough to vote for them, so the seducer has to conclude that the woman who falls in love with him is not only a fool, but also, by definition, unworthy of everything except a share of his self-contempt which he will cheerfully pass along as if it were a little dose of clap.

George Garrett, *Poison Pen*

That may be a bit of a cynical charac-
terization, and a bit verbose, but here is one
that is at least more concise:

«»

*We are selected by mates during a phase,
and the phase frequently passes.*

Jim Harrison, Julip

Sometimes the attraction is a mystery, perhaps some sort of magic, or a Darwinian survival mechanism:

《》

...and when you're informed that a person likes you, your instinctive response is to like the person back.

Paul Auster, *Invisible*

But even if all the confusion is overcome and a relationship develops, men and women may soon encounter some challenges:

«◊»

The difficulty with women is that their feelings are apt to get interested sooner than ours, and then, you know, reasoning is out of the question.

Bret Harte, "The Man of No Account"

Once the relationship is underway (please excuse the nautical term), communication becomes important to its success or failure. Here are a couple of examples:

«»

Let her be soft-spoken, also, if you please. For there's nothing like a shrill and nagging woman to put a man, even a Protestant, into an early purgatory.

George Garrett, *The Succession*

Another author's character offers some advice about how to avoid trouble in communication:

《》

There was also the good tough rule that said that telling one's female anything at all about your dealings with another was to be avoided whenever possible.

Kingsley Amis, Jake's Thing

If communications are successful, or at least do not doom the relationship, it may prosper. Authors and their characters have offered some approaches that may be viable:

«»

Well, I had not calculated to alienate her permanently—the only way to live with a woman is in amity.

Wallace Stegner,
All the Little Live Things

Here is a very similar sentiment with a creative metaphor:

《》

A man has to be patient with women. Like stalking a covey of birds. Beginnings are rocky sometimes but when you least expect it things smooth out.

John Dos Passos, *The Great Days*

If, however, things do not "smooth out," and they get worse, a warning is in order, perhaps like this one that a well-known and well-regarded American author's character delivers, with a striking metaphor, to the novel's main character:

«»

Beware of women in crises... They're like flypaper. Even if you tear yourself away you leave a wing in their stickiness.

William Kennedy, The Ink Truck

From the woman's perspective, men may offer some value in the relationship, but there may be a delicate balance between her man's being an asset or a liability:

«»

A little incapacity in a man can be charming. Like not being able to tie a bow tie. Complete helplessness is another matter altogether.

John Casey, *Compass Rose*

One of the more stereotypical male traits may be a plus for some women:

«»

Men for all their hidden rage did have that—a plain sense of cause and effect, a practical desire to be reasonable. Women love them for that.

John Updike, *The Widows of Eastwick*

None of this guarantees long-term success for the relationship. Here is a cynical view from a character in a novel by an author who has been successful in print, on the radio, and on stage:

«»

A woman can make you happy for about ten minutes a week, and that's it. The rest of the time you're on your own.

Garrison Keillor, *Wobegon Boy*

A famous (or infamous) British playwright expresses his dismay at a perceived female characteristic:

«»

Egad! I might be married to her; she treats me with such darned indifference.

Oscar Wilde, *Lady Windemere's Fan*

An American director and author had one of his characters use a powerful metaphor to express frustration with a rocky relationship:

«»

We were living on islands, the bridge between us was burning, and no one was trying to put it out.

Elia Kazan, The Understudy

The conflicts, the mismatch, may be insufferable. A popular contemporary author's character tries to explain it:

«»

There's a certain man, an archetype, he's a model of dependability for his male friends, all the things a friend should be, an ally and confidant, lends money, gives advice, loyal and so on, but sheer hell on women. Living, breathing hell. The closer a woman gets, the clearer it becomes to him that she is not one of his male friends. And the more awful it becomes for her.

Don DeLillo, *Falling Man*

And there are some ironies that make the success of the relationship a challenge. Here are a couple of examples. The first is from a very highly regarded Irish author:

《》

No one told him that keeping the faith could be as cruel as confessing faithlessness;...

William Trevor, "Old Flame,"
Cheating at Canasta

The second is from a very popular American female author:

«»

Sometimes she thought the trouble was, she and Leon were too well acquainted. The most innocent remark could call up such a string of associations, so many past slights and insults never quite settled or forgotten, merely smoothed over. They could no longer have a single uncomplicated feeling about each other.

Anne Tyler, Morgan's Passing

Even the relationships that have some legs have their ups and downs over time. Here is a good description, with a creative metaphor, of the phenomenon:

《》

—a view of my years…(of our years together) as a stream that splits from time to time for durations of various lengths, some brief, some painfully sustained, into two smaller streams, then reunites, splits and reunites, with happy recognition, despite any amount of babbling and gurgling, of gained power, of gained breadth and depth in each reunion.

Dennis McFarland,
A Face at the Window

Here is another description, sans metaphor, by a famous and very prolific American author:

«»

Well, these things wax and wane—detachment and tenderness, incredible tenderness and then incredible inaccessibility, that's the pattern with people who've stuck together as long as we have.

Philip Roth, *Deception*

A few authors have had their characters express some fundamental skepticism about the ultimate chances for a happy or successful romantic relationship:

《》

Let's face it, a new woman stands for a new life, that's why men are always after them. The women don't like to think about that. A man falls for somebody and it's about escape nine times out of ten; the tenth maybe it's cooking.

Frederick Barthelme,
The Natural Selection

And the ultimate irony may be this one, expressed by a character in a story by one of America's finest authors:

《》

It's after all the woman you didn't *have whose effect is mortal.*

Saul Bellow, "Cousins,"
Him With His Foot in His Mouth

I seriously contemplated whether this section should precede or follow the next one. Sometimes, the order of events in a relationship is love, then sex; in other cases, it is sex, then love, and maybe sometimes, both at once. In any case, with all due respect to the other order, I chose this one.

Regardless of the order of love and sex between two people, each participant in the relationship probably has some conscious or, at least, subconscious idea of what love is. That idea may be well-developed, well-considered, and reasonable, or none of these. Given the differences between men and women, it should come as no surprise that their respective notions of love may differ significantly. It may be helpful if their ideas of love are similar, but similar perspectives may not be necessary for a long-lasting, satisfying relationship.

Some relationships do not last, but others blossom and mature, with one or (preferably both) finding love. A lot may depend upon how they define "love."

Here is a rather complicated notion from a well-known British author:

«»

For either you're in love with the woman or you aren't; either you're carried away by your inflamed imagination (for, after all, the person you're really violently in love with is always your own invention and the wildest of fancies) or by your senses and your intellectual curiosity.... But if you are, it means that you become enslaved, involved, dependent on another human being in a way that's positively disgraceful, and the more disgraceful the more there is in you to be enslaved and involved.

Aldous Huxley, *Those Barren Leaves*

Another British author is quite discursive and descriptive on the topic.

«»

That [love] is an emotion in which tenderness is an essential part...there is in love a sense of weakness, a desire to protect, an eagerness to do good and to give pleasure—if not unselfishness, at all events a selfishness which marvelously conceals itself; it has in it a certain diffidence... Love is absorbing; it takes the lover out of himself; the most clear-sighted, though he may know, cannot realize that this love will cease; it gives body to what he knows is illusion, and, knowing it is nothing else, he loves it better than reality. It makes a man a little more than himself, and at the same time a little less. He ceases to be himself. He is no longer an individual, but a thing, an instrument to some purpose foreign to his ego. Love is never quite devoid of sentimentality...

W. Somerset Maugham,
The Moon and Sixpence

A third British writer has a shorter, but still pessimistic, perspective on love:

«»

To be in love is to see yourself as someone else sees you, it is to be in love with the falsified and exalted image of yourself. In love we are incapable of honour—the courageous act is no more than playing a part to an audience of two.

Graham Greene, The Quiet American

How about an American, that is, US, perspective that might be a bit more positive?

«»

...it will be lonesome without her. Is that what love is? The recognition that life will be less, that it will be a huge loss to be without the one you love? And maybe the knowledge that all the time before, the life you had before you fell in love, was wasted time. Love is a time of brightness bracketed by losses on both sides.

George Garrett, *The King of Babylon Shall Not Come Against You*

Here is a suggestion about an ingredient of love:

«»

Mystery in a person is attractive: more often than not it is its presence that inspires the helpless, tumbling descent into love.

William Trevor, *Death in Summer*

A prolific author known for his stories involving affairs of love and/or lust has a short metaphor to offer:

《》

I remembered the longing that our poor minds press against the bodies of others, like water against bodies of swimmers.

John Updike, *Roger's Version*

Here is an advocate of the concept that love is "all in your mind":

«◊»

Lovers live in each other's minds.

E. L. Doctorow, Andrew's Brain

One of the shortest and most positive thoughts comes from a Czech-born writer who has lived in exile since 1975 in France:

«»

...and love is the glorification of the present.

Milan Kundera, *Ignorance*

Of course, some men have a much more cynical view of love. Leave it to this author, who knows how to turn a phrase, to make an unusual comparison:

«»

I also assumed I still loved her, but then love can be a routine, like farming.

Jim Harrison, *The English Major*

However love may be defined, some men have a bit of a self-centered view of their roles:

《》

As much as a man may love or hate himself (and usually it is a blending of both together in us all), there's no man who doesn't imagine that he is worthy of the love and admiration of women.

George Garrett, The Succession

Some may yearn for love long before they find it:

《》

...for I have no particular appeal to women, only to this woman, and so the recognition must be mutual and it pushes us toward each other despite our differences, and our inability to understand each other's language, and here it has happened again though I am indisputably older, fatter, and more ridiculous as a figure of love than I have been before. Always I am older. Always we do not understand each other. Always I lose her. Oh God who made this girl give her to me this time to hold let me sink into the complacencies of fulfilled love, let us lose our memories together, and let me die from the ordinary insubstantial results of having lived.

E. L. Doctorow, Loon Lake

After searching and yearning for love, a man, or woman, may place a very high value on it:

«»

If you're lucky enough to fall in love, that's one thing. Otherwise, all that was ever truly beautiful to me was boyhood. It's the meal we sup on for the rest of our lives. Love puts the icing on life. But if you don't find it…you must call on your childhood memories over and over till you do.

Leon Uris, *Trinity*

But here again, there may be significant differences between men and women in love:

«»

No man can love like a woman can, they don't have the internal organs for it.

John Updike, *The Widows of Eastwick*

So, does fate or luck have a role in finding love? At least one character seems to think so:

《》

To have someone you love know you better than you know yourself is a compliment;.... When someone knows your deepest self and still loves you, are you not a lucky man?

Richard Russo, *Bridge of Sighs*

High valuations of love may generate high expectations to be fulfilled—or not:

«»

You expected such a damned lot from love, a unique excitement, a quality of everlastingness, no value remained unshaken when love was this...

Graham Greene, *It's a Battlefield*

It is natural to expect that the early phase of love would be rewarding. Here is a great expression of the first impression. If my memory serves me, I've had at least one such experience:

《》

There is no moment that exceeds in beauty that moment when one looks at a woman and finds that she is looking at you in the same way that you are looking at her.... The initial smash on glance.

Donald Barthelme, "The Sea of Hesitation," *Overnight to Many Distant Cities*

Just because love starts off "with a bang" does not mean all will be well:

«»

When a man falls in love it's ninety to one he falls for the dame that's worst for him.

John Steinbeck, *Sweet Thursday*

Time goes on, and things are bound to change, for better or, in this somewhat cynical view, for worse:

«»

...love, insofar as he understood it, depended on a thing remaining forever what it was, which in [his] experience it militantly refused to do. What people called love was the perfect recipe for disappointment and recrimination at the benign end of the emotional spectrum, homicide at the malignant end.

Richard Russo, *Bridge of Sighs*

A famous Mexican author's character seems to agree wholeheartedly:

《》

The first passion is never recaptured. On the other hand, regret stays with us forever. Remorse. Lament. It turns to melancholy and lives in us like a frustrated ghost.

Carlos Fuentes, Inez

Putting aside these rather dire assumptions or predictions, it is natural that there will be issues to be addressed. Here is a very good explanation of a fundamental one:

《》

It's natural to want someone you love to do what you want, or what you think would be good for them, but you have to let everything happen to them. You can't interfere with people you love any more than you're supposed to interfere with people you don't even know. And that's hard…because you often feel like interfering—you want to be the one who makes the plans.

John Irving, *Cider House Rules*

This famous and very popular British author explores another recurring potential problem:

«»

If only it were possible to love without injury—fidelity is not enough:...the hurt is in the act of possession; we are too small in mind and body to possess another person without pride or to be possessed without humiliation.

Graham Greene, The Quiet American

The next warning, if you will, comes from a very successful Irish novelist and short story writer:

«»

Because love nourished instinct, and instinct's short cuts and economies, too much had been too carelessly left.

William Trevor, *The Story of Lucy Gault*

As we get older, complications may increase, or at least increase in importance:

«»

The problem with middle-aged love is that its seriousness rises in proportion to its lack of reality. If you think a woman has fallen in love with an inflated image of you, you'd much rather break your neck than not live up to it.

Jules Feiffer,
Harry, The Rat With Women

Perhaps a dose of realism is in order for those who are seeking love or who think they have found it. The character in this author's novel puts in very concisely:

«»

But even love can't see clearly over the curve of the earth.

Ivan Doig, *Dancing at the Rascal Fair*

Sex

Whichever comes first, love or sex, sexual relations have received a large volume of commentary in literature, and not just in romance novels. Some reviewers have claimed that modern and contemporary novels, stories, and plays (to say nothing about movies and television shows) contain "gratuitous sex." Maybe so, but we should acknowledge that sex has historically been an important enough subject that it has found its way into literature for centuries. Older works may have treated sex a bit more subtly than more modern works, but it has been there nonetheless. These quotes consider the relationship between love and sex, and the role of sex in relationships.

This famous, and very highly regarded, Canadian author offers a serious observation, with a humorous touch:

«»

It was all quite different in my day. Love was an emotion greatly valued, but it was valued for its own sake, and an unhappy love or a torturing love was perhaps even more valued than a love that was fulfilled. After all, love is an ecstasy, but sex is an appetite, and one does not always satisfy an appetite at the best restaurant in town.

Robertson Davies, *The Lyre of Orpheus*

One character explains how his concept of love may have been intertwined with sex:

«»

...I wished to know no other woman in that special way, and I wonder whether that cannot be described as a kind of love: the sexual preference for one person above all others.

V. S. Naipaul, *Magic Seeds*

According to some, sex lights a fire in the relationship. Again, a little humor helps make the point:

«»

Wait till you get to sex... It's a grand surprise nature has cooked up for us, love with its accelerated pulse and its drastic overestimation of the love object, its rhythmic build-up and discharge; but then that's it, there isn't another such treat life can offer, unless you count contract bridge and death.

John Updike, Roger's Version

Sex, by itself, may lead to mutual love—or not:

«»

In general, when you felt a longing for love, you took a woman and possessed her gingerly and not too hopefully until you finally let go, slept, woke up and she eluded you once more. Then you started over. Or not.

Lorrie Moore,
"What You Want to Do Fine,"
Birds of America

As with love, expectations for sex may be too high:

《》

And it was the rock-bottom puzzlement of life and time: there is an ideal woman who will return to you the kind of sexual life you could have had at nineteen but didn't. That this was not meant to be for men on Earth did not stop millions of fools from looking.

Jim Harrison, Julip

Here is a thoughtful suggestion that there may be more to sex than physical connection:

«»

He wonders if words aren't an essential element of sex, if talking isn't finally a more subtle form of touching, and if the images dancing in our heads aren't just as important as the bodies we hold in our arms.

Paul Auster, *Invisible*

For others, sex is playing a role:

«»

...most sex was acting anyway.
John Updike, The Widows of Eastwick

Whether filled with pretense or genuine, sex can lead to a state of affairs that is less than blissful. Here is a concise description of what sex can do that, perhaps, it should not:

«»

I know that every mistake that a man can make usually has a sexual accelerator.

Philip Roth, *The Human Stain*

And there may be costs to be paid for the sex, and the costs may or may not be payable all in cash or by credit card:

«»

You sleep with somebody in a moment of truth and the obligations begin to pile up nightmarishly.

John Updike, *Roger's Version*

It is, I guess, for each to decide if the costs are worth it. Here is how one of my all-time favorite writers had a character express his assessment:

«»

I had always believed, and not only out of cynicism, that a man and a woman could tell in the first ten minutes whether they wanted to go to bed together; and that the time that passed after those first ten minutes represented a tax, which might be worth paying if the article promised to be really enjoyable, but which nine times out of ten became rapidly excessive.

John Fowles, *The Magus*

Some appear to be beyond cynicism on the subject:

«»

Sexuality had so many layers and those at the bottom were pathetic.

Jim Harrison, *The Great Leader*

The risks and costs of sex within the relationship are one thing, but the risks and costs increase pretty significantly with sex outside the relationship:

«»

The sexual coupling of an older man and younger woman, especially one not his marriage partner, was apparently only a little less deadly than cyanide.

John Gardner, *Mickelsson's Ghosts*

Even so, some men seem to thrive on extracurricular sexual engagement:

«»

A piece of village wisdom he was slow to grasp is that sex is a holiday, an activity remarkably brief in our body's budget compared with sleeping or food-gathering or constructing battlements for self-defense, such as the Great Wall of China. The unfaithful man and woman meet for a plain purpose, dangerous and scandalous, with the blood pressure up and the pupils enlarged and the love-flesh already reddening the skin: is there not a praiseworthy economy in this, as opposed to sex spread thin through the interminable mutual exposure of marriage?

John Updike, *Villages*

Here is, perhaps, a more balanced, realistic assessment:

«»

The thing about you and your wife making love was that it made things all right, not often for ever but always for a time and always for longer than the actual love-making. In that it was unique: adultery could make life more interesting but it couldn't make things all right in a month of Sundays.

Kingsley Amis, Jake's Thing

The next idea may seem a bit old-fashioned, coming as it does from a character in this author's novel, but that does not mean there is no truth in it:

«»

...this illicit love-making is the one game you always lose at. If you do lose, you feel foolish; and if you win, as soon as you find out how little it is that you've been scheming for, why then you lose worse than ever.

Sinclair Lewis, *Main Street*

A counterpoint, to some extent, is this old saw:

«»

...screwing your wife is like striking out the pitcher.

William Kennedy, *Billy Phelan's Greatest Game*

With all these differing views of the role of sex in relationships, it may be safe to say there are some unanswered questions. This might be an apt conclusion:

«»

Who am I that I should seek to unravel the mysterious intricacies of sex?

W. Somerset Maugham,
The Moon and Sixpence

Marriage

Despite all the real and imagined differences between men and women, some enter into serious (or not so serious) relationships, some fall in love and/or engage in sex, and whether it is because of the love, sex, or something else, such as money, social status, or culinary talent, some marry. It would not be an exaggeration to suggest that no two marriages are exactly alike. (*Snowflakes maybe, but marriages?*) In addition, it seems natural and, perhaps in some cases, advantageous, that marriages change over time. These features make marriages a fertile topic for writers of literary fiction, and their observations span quite a range of positive and negative perspectives.

Some men search for a long time to find the perfect match.

Women, beware of men who are unsuccessful:

«»

Men traveling alone develop a romantic vertigo.

John Updike, *Bech: A Book*

Maybe it's like traveling, getting there is most, or all, of the fun. That seems to be the gist of this dialogue:

《》

One doesn't want the search to end.

Just so. For example, I've been thinking about getting a new wristwatch. For the last ten years. Everywhere I travel, I look at wristwatches in shop windows. Seen a great many splendid wristwatches. Were I to actually buy *a new wristwatch, one of my most pleasant diversions would be denied me.*

One could apply the same logic to wives.

Donald Barthelme, The King

Some never find the marriageable mate. For this character, it was, perhaps, a wise choice:

«»

He never married, you know. He always said that by the time he knew the woman well enough to marry her, he knew better.

John Steinbeck,
The Short Reign of Pippin IV

Many men apparently have poor criteria for the selection process. Here is an excellent metaphor for a poor basis for choosing a mate:

《》

Marrying a woman for her beauty makes no more sense than eating a bird for its singing. But it's a common mistake nonetheless.

Charles Frazier, Cold Mountain

To make the odds for men even worse, some women believe the institution of marriage is not to be trusted. This female character is adamant on the topic:

«»

Matrimony, she explained, was based on two fallacies, both real doozies. The first was the ridiculous notion that people knew what they wanted. There was no evidence in support of this contention and never had been, but they seemed to enjoy believing it anyway, blinded as they were by love, and lust, and hope, only the last of which sprang eternal. The second fallacy, built on the shifting sands of the first, was equally seductive and even more idiotic—that what people thought they wanted today was what they'd want tomorrow.

Richard Russo, Bridge of Sighs

Another female character had a more complex, but very discerning, idea of marriage. How true!

«»

Marriage, she felt, was a fine arrangement generally, except that one never got it generally. One got it specifically, very specifically.

Lorrie Moore, "Real Estate,"
Birds of America

In some marriages, love, at least as one character understood it, may be missing:

«»

I do not suppose she had ever really cared for her husband, and what I had taken for love was no more than the feminine response to caresses and comfort which the minds of most women passes for it.

W. Somerset Maugham,
The Moon and Sixpence

So, it seems marriage is no sure thing:

«»

Marriage was an uncalculated risk... The trickiest of all undertakings...

William Trevor, "Cheating at Canasta," *Cheating at Canasta*

As with premarital relationships between men and women, the quality of communications, or lack thereof, may be a key factor in the success and happiness of a marriage:

«»

Overheard, or recorded, all marital conversation sounds as if someone must be joking, though usually no one is.

Lorrie Moore, "People Like That Are the Only People Here," *Birds of America*

If men would just be a little smarter about what topics they discuss with their wives, maybe more love would survive:

《》

Married men don't assert themselves, not if they know what's good for them.

P. G. Wodehouse,
The Plot that Thickened

As one might expect, a marriage may start out quite well, but go downhill sooner or later. In this case, the view expressed is that is likely to be sooner:

«»

That was near the end of the honeymoon, the typical ninety days of passion before the grim reality of domestic bliss begins to sink into the mutual consciousness of man and wife.

Edward Abbey, *The Fool's Progress*

Most marriages will encounter problems. Is this a common one?

«»

What is marriage without exploitation? People in marriages get exploited a million times over. One exploits the other's position, one exploits the other's money, one exploits the other's looks.

Philip Roth, I Married a Communist

If not exploitation, how about a related vice: manipulation?

《》

It is part of the art of marriage of wives and husbands to manipulate their spouses' moods—wives with food, husbands with flowers, and both at times with an affected languor. Moreover, it usually works, even if one is conscious of the other's calculation….

Piers Paul Read, *A Season in the West*

It would be foolish not to expect some ups and downs. Here is a somewhat pessimistic perspective from a Nobel Prize-winning German author:

«»

It'll drag on like every marriage, sometimes better, sometimes worse...marital crises, marital quarrels, marital infidelity! An evergreen topic.

Günter Grass, *Too Far Afield*

Even some interactions that should be constructive may turn out otherwise:

«»

Nothing kills a marriage like social intercourse. The man goes to work in the morning, comes home as late as he can, exhausted, disgruntled, and loaded with every excuse for not making any contact but the most elementary.

Imagine what would happen...if the husband stayed home all day.

Elia Kazan, The Understudy

Some people claim there is no such thing as a successful or happy marriage:

«»

"Oh, there's no such thing as a successful marriage," she said. "There are marriages that give up and marriages that keep on trying; that's the only difference."

Garrison Keillor, Wobegon Boy

That negative view may depend on the definition of "successful." If one's sights are set low enough, success may be achievable:

《》

You know what a marriage is? It's either a housekeeping arrangement or a power struggle.

Alan Lightman, Ghost

There are, of course, any number of reasons for marriages to fail, and these seem very credible:

«»

"Our marriage failed for lack of fun;"… Fun is the only way to survive. A marriage is doomed without it. Think of all the time you have to spend alone, the pair of you. You have to renew, renew, renew. It's time that wrecks marriages, obviously.

Don DeLillo, *Ratner's Star*

Could this be another—a fundamental problem or just an individual one?

«»

She could not pause to see objectively that no man's wife,…was not dull in comparison to the sprightlier object of his newest adulterous infatuation.

Joseph Heller,
Portrait of an Artist, as an Old Man

Yet, some, at least a few, seem to find formulae for success:

《》

...but I decided—I think on the whole wisely—that a profound understanding between spouses was not essential to a happy marriage.

Louis Auchincloss, Honourable Men

This one may not work for everyone, but it could be worth a try. After all, it is the spirit that counts, not the legalities:

«»

Of course she was my wife, but we never married. We never got around to it. We never got past the intense feeling for each other that you have to get past in order to legally marry. We didn't need anyone else to tell us we were.

E. L. Doctorow, *Andrew's Brain*

Divorce does not, in general, seem to help one's perspective on marriage. An unconventional author's character describes in very visual terms the effect of divorce on him:

《》

I've been in divorce court five times. Do you know what that does to you? When I look into a young girl's eyes for the first time, I seem to see her lawyer staring back at me.

William Kotzwinkle, *The Exile*

So, it may be that men are to blame for a fundamental failure to adapt successfully to the institution of marriage:

《》

It's after all the woman you didn't have whose effect is mortal.

Saul Bellow, "Cousins,"
Him With His Foot in His Mouth

Few will argue against all of the differences between men and women described in the quotes here. We have explored only some notable examples. Despite their differences, many men and women find and maintain valuable romantic relationships, some with more love and/or sex than others. That is not to say that all those that last are mutually satisfying, to the same or any degree, for the men and women, but many do last an adult lifetime. Fate or luck may play a role, perhaps even a more important role than motivation, in the outcome.

I would like to express my deep appreciation for all the hard work by Tyson Cornell and his staff at Rare Bird, especially Alice Marsh-Elmer, whose creativity is evident in the book's design. I would also like to thank Pat Walsh, who believed in the literary value of my personal collection of quotations and brought together the talents necessary for successful publication of this book.